The
Devil's Grimoire
A System of Psychic Attack

Winter Tempest
Books

Moribus Mortlock

2013
Winter Tempest Books

ISBN: 0615891837
ISBN-13: 978-0615891835
Winter Tempest Books

DEDICATION

In honor of my grandparents.

Contents

ABOUT THE DEVIL'S GRIMOIRE

This volume introduces you to 36 little devils you can employ to attack your enemies while guarding and benefiting yourself. It is an entire system of psychic attack, which includes provisions for your own defense. These little devils are egregores, which are sophisticated thought-forms with limited intelligence, programmed to carry out specific actions when they are activated. By using this system, people who need more control over their own lives may attain it; both minor nuisances and major problems may be eliminated.

While you will find numerous books on the subject of psychic self-defense, it is more unusual to find a book that shows you how to launch a psychic attack. Many occultists are unwilling to share this information, fearing that it might be abused should it land in the hands of an immoral or unethical person.

But, the author of this book differs on this point; he believes that humanity has a right to such knowledge. Furthermore, he believes that you have the right to defend yourself from those who create difficulties for you. You have a right to both peace and justice. Therefore, this book was written to help you obtain these things without incurring any risk to yourself.

In an ideal world, there would always be kindness, fairness, respect, justice and security. But, this is not a perfect world, which is why *The Devil's Grimoire* is needed.

Not having the ability to defend ourselves or obtain justice can render a sense of fear and helplessness in us. Moreover, it is wrong to expect someone who has been grievously wronged to simply turn the other cheek and move forward without the ability to re-establish balance in their lives. Such an expectation is not only unrealistic, but cruel.

It is a fact of life that sometimes trouble finds you through no fault of your own and when this happens, you must bring a swift end to it to maintain your peace of mind and go about your life's purpose unimpeded. This is why the author of this book will never shake a moralizing finger at you, cast judgment on you or caution you about the perils of using of this information, rather it is assumed that you are in control of your own life and have good motivations for whatever you do.

Succeeding at psychic attack is not a matter of belief or faith, nor is it a matter of simply thinking certain thoughts, wishing or intending to do something. Rather, there is a procedure, which must be followed in order to obtain consistent and tangible results.

It is not enough to simply read this book and take no

action. To prevail against your enemies and ultimately attain a high degree of psychic self-defense in the process, you must conduct your own personal experiments with the procedures presented herein.

So, do not just read this book and cast it aside whether because of doubt or for any other reason, but put this information to use. Once you demonstrate to yourself that you can do it, you will be empowered, inspired and encouraged to expand on your abilities.

Moribus Mortlock

HOW TO USE THE DEVIL'S GRIMOIRE

The little devils may be employed in an unlimited variety of situations with the stipulation that you should not use them against people who live under your own roof. The first 33 are unpleasant spirits, who may be invoked and dispatched at your discretion. The final three are guardians.

In order to prove to yourself the efficacy of this system, conduct your first experiments with enemies who are close at hand, for example, a noisy neighbor or a troublesome co-worker.

When you are sure of your ability to make the spirits work for you, then you will be able to confidently dispatch them on missions at a greater distance. Once you see that you are able to effectively employ them by observing the behavior of enemies close at hand, you can rest assured that enemies at a greater distance are being affected in a similar way.

Examples of how the little devils may be used:

To end problems with co-workers
To deal with a bad manager or boss
To put a stop to gossip and slander
To eliminate a competitor in business, love, etc.
To obtain revenge on someone who has harmed you
To obtain justice in the courts
To end abuse by those in positions of power and authority
To stop bullies
To stop criminals
To dominate enemies and bring them under your will
To stop someone who is harassing or threatening you
To strike at enemies from a distance

Preparation for Conjuring the Little Devils

It is likely that anyone who has an interest in psychic attack has a personal reason for pursuing this subject. It may be that you have been harmed by someone or you require protection from dangerous people. In such cases as these, especially severe ones, you may be feeling highly emotional, in particular, you may feel resentment and rage toward your enemy. This is not necessarily a bad thing.

Anger can help you in your workings, especially against someone who has deeply wronged you, but it will help you most when you bring it under your control and condense its energy. If you have ever been able to make something extraordinary happen to an enemy when you were angry, then you know how powerful the condensed, directed energy of anger can be. But, anger tainted with frustration or fear renders you weak and helpless.

Feelings of fear and frustration can be difficult to completely overcome, however, if you are to succeed at psychic attack, you must do so, at least, long enough to complete the procedure. Afterward, you may resume feeling fearful and frustrated, if you like.

For a short period of time, you must be able to focus on your meditation, the purpose of which is to condense and direct a powerful energy force from within you. You must do this in a safe, quiet place where you are able to be undisturbed.

Achieve a meditative state by any method you are accustomed to. If you do not have an established method of your own, simply sit comfortably in an upright position, close your eyes and visualize the color black. See the darkest, most pure shade of black you can conjure before your mind's eye. Once you have achieved this, count backward slowly from "10" to "1." Then, take one or two deep breaths as you allow yourself to sink into a dream-like state.

To prepare for conjuring and dispatching the little devils, practice holding complex images in your mind for, at least, a minute or two. For example, memorize photographs of people, rooms or other locations. The more accurate the image you can hold in your mind the better because the memory possesses an energetic pattern which has the same value as the person or location it represents.

Once you are able to achieve this meditative state and hold fairly complex images in your mind, you will easily be able to conjure and dispatch the entities.

How to Conjure the Little Devils

There are two methods of conjuring and employing these spirits: The first is a hands-on, more practical method and the second is a mental method. Choose either one according to your abilities and the amount of access you have to your enemy.

Regardless of which method you use, you must attain a meditative state at the time you conjure and direct the beings to your enemy.

Note: The incantations are written in the male gender. If your enemy is a woman alter them accordingly. Specific commands to the spirits are entirely optional.

1. The Practical Method:

On a small, clean piece of parchment or white paper, draw the sigil of the spirit you wish to conjure.

Then, place it over the top of a personal effect of the enemy. A personal effect may be a photograph, which is a full-body shot in which the person is the sole subject; a spot of blood or bodily fluids; a piece of soiled underwear; hairs from the person's head or body; a signature; a personal item the enemy frequently carries next to his skin; or nail clippings. If you lack this, write the person's name and birth date, if you know it, on a small piece of clean parchment or white paper and use this.

Wrap the sigil and the personal effect together with a black cord and tie it fast.

Place your palms down over this item and recite the incantation associated with that spirit while visualizing the being according to its description and seeing the spirit go out to attach itself to your enemy.

If you are conjuring and dispatching multiple entities to an enemy, wrap the sigil of each spirit around this personal effect and recite the associated conjuration in succession, layering one on top of the other.

2. The Mental Method:

Place the sigil of the spirit you wish to conjure before you.

Go into a meditative state.

Read the description of the spirit and formulate an image in your mind of what this being looks like and what he does.

Picture your enemy, re-create the sound of his voice in your head, see the movements he makes when he walks or speaks, which are uniquely his. Locate his energetic pattern by whatever means. If you know what the inside of his home or business looks like, use this information to mentally locate the energetic form of his body.

Recite the incantation for the spirit. Envision the spirit, not before you, but attached to your enemy. See the being performing his function and sustain this visualization for as long as you can, preferably 10 or 15 minutes.

How to Employ the Little Devils

In any situation, determine what outcome you desire. Then, consider which of the little devils in *Chapter 4* can best help you achieve this end. It is often beneficial to dispatch multiple spirits to act as a team.

Some of the spirits are of an obsessive nature, some are possessive and some are both. Obsessive spirits cause the enemy to become the victim of external forces and the actions of others. By contrast, possessive spirits take control of the enemy's mind, body and emotions and cause him to behave in unnatural ways.

The demon, Fejund, multiplies into a pack, but multiple instances of any of these little devils can be dispatched to overwhelm an enemy.

There is no need to wait for any particular time to communicate with these spirits. They will gleefully perform their duties regardless of the time of day or night. A spirit may be dispatched to more than one enemy at a time because each time one is sent out, it makes an energetic copy of itself. The being will survive as long as it has an energy supply.

The more you know about your enemy and his psychology and existing weaknesses, the better you can determine which little devils to employ in a given situation. For example, if you have an enemy who has weak health, a weak mind, is in some way reckless or who naturally has violent or criminal tendencies, then dispatch spirits according to his condition and inclinations. You can still succeed knowing very little about your enemy, but any information you have in this regard may be of use to you.

Demonstrate to yourself the efficacy of these little devils by trying them out on enemies that are close at hand, whose activities are observable to you, such as co-workers or neighbors. Although, it is not recommended to employ them against people living in your own home.

Generally, the spirits are happy as long as they have a living host. They don't really care who the host is and, as long as they have a food supply, they will continue to plague their victim until their purpose is completely carried out.

Nonetheless, if the entity runs out of food, there is a chance he may return to you. Therefore, you must employ the guardians. After you dispatch any one of these spirits, summon and charge your guardians as described in *Chapter 5*.

Be advised that it is easier to begin an operation than to stop it once it has begun, so before you begin any undertaking involving these spirits be certain of what you want to accomplish.

See *Chapter 5* for more information about managing or stopping a psychic attack operation.

Moribus Mortlock

EXAMPLES OF EFFECTIVE STRATEGIES FOR EMPLOYING THE LITTLE DEVILS

The following hypothetical scenarios illustrate strategies for dispatching the little devils:

The Noisy Neighbors

Regardless of where you live, suddenly one day you may find yourself plagued by neighbors who play loud music or throw wild parties at all hours. There is usually no good, practical way to deal with this problem. Confronting them could be dangerous and calling the police will probably only get you labeled as a trouble-maker while doing nothing to end your misery. In a situation like this, the little devils will be your best friends.

Choose one or more spirits from the list of 33 in *Chapter 4* with the intention of sickening, terrorizing and driving the trouble-makers out. You might choose a combination of Colonius, Ferracco and, since you are having problems with people in a particular place, Dompravus.

Perhaps you have a photograph of the miscreants or their home, which you have taken without their knowledge, of course. If you have such a thing, you may apply it using the practical method of conjuring and dispatching the little devils. If you know what your neighbors look like, then you have this energetic pattern to work with mentally. But, even if you have not seen the people, if you can hear them and their noise, you can locate them mentally.

If you have been suffering very long from the actions of these neighbors, you may be feeling very frustrated. You may, also, find that it is difficult for your to concentrate, especially, if the noise is very loud. But, to succeed, you must briefly lose your frustration and maintain your focus on your work.

Be confident that you will soon bring an end to your suffering by this method. Knowing that you are not helpless, will help you let go of some of your frustration. If the noise is so loud you cannot effectively concentrate, go to the quietest place in your home or put in some earplugs for the duration of this operation. It should not take long to disperse your noise-makers.

Go into a calm, focused meditative state. Once you have achieved this, perform the conjuration of the first of the spirits and see him attached to your enemy.

Warning: Never conjure any of the 33 spirits in *Chapter 4* to you, but always see them at a distance obsessing and possessing your enemy.

See this first spirit, Colonius, attached to one of your enemies. You may dispatch more than one instance of this being by repeating the conjuration and, thereby, sicken an entire party. You must maintain your focus in this meditative state and actually see Colonius entering the body of your enemies, making them very ill. It may take ten or fifteen minutes, but in a short time, they should become very quiet.

When this happens, you may either cease or continue your working. If you cease immediately, they may start the noise, again, in a little while after they have recovered. For this reason, you may want to maintain this intense visualization for a while after they become quiet.

This operation should end their fun for the night, but if they are very determined to make a nuisance of themselves, you will have to drive them out. The next time they make noise, mentally speak to Colonius and tell him to do his job. Visualize him sickening the party and when the noise stops and they have retired for the night, send Ferracco to torment them in their beds. Again, go into your meditative state, conjure the spirit, strongly envision this shadowy cloaked, stiletto-wielding figure and let him loose on your enemies.

You may conjure the third demon now or wait to see if they persist in their noise-making. The third spirit chosen in this example is Dompravus, who will terrorize and sicken anyone who enters your enemy's house. Again, go into a meditative state, conjure and dispatch Dompravus and see him working for 10 or 15 minutes.

You may have to perform these conjurations a few times to reinforce your point, but soon you will notice that the noisy neighbors have suddenly become very quiet. They may be sick, they may be staying elsewhere most of the time or they have abandoned the dwelling.

The Bully Boss

Like the noisy neighbors, the bully boss is a good example of the type of enemy to experiment with before you move on to instances involving more distant enemies. In a case like this one, not only will you have the opportunity to observe the effect of your psychic attack, you will likely have more opportunity to consider the psychology and natural tendencies of your enemy and what weaknesses you might exploit. For example, ask yourself what negative characteristics he possesses that you might exacerbate, thus accelerating his downfall.

Let us suppose you have a boss who is a sociopathic bully. In this particular instance, he is not only psychologically cruel to you and your co-workers, but you have the idea that he might be doing something unethical, although you have no actual proof of this.

In this case, you are likely to have a photograph or some other personal effect of your boss, which you can apply to the practical method or you may use the entirely mental method. Whichever method you choose, it is best to work your witchcraft outside the office, although you can reinforce the hold the spirits have on your enemy whenever you feel like it.

Begin by selecting one or spirits from the list of 33. For this example, we will employ Corpo, Malfatum and Malgojo.

After a day of being tormented by your tyrannical boss, go home and relax, confident in the fact that you are going to take control of this situation. Go into a meditative state and conjure the first spirit, Corpo. See this spirit by your boss' side, then see him take complete possession of his body. Focus for 10 or 15 minutes on this visualization, seeing this spirit inside the boss, taking over his entire personality as he becomes a greedy glutton with sticky fingers.

Over the course of the next two or three days, watch to see if your boss has changed his behavior in any way. At this point, there is probably no noticeable change, so on the next day of aggravation, go home, then go into your meditative state and conjure and dispatch Malfatum, an obsessive spirit who brings down the high and mighty and causes those once favored to be spurned.

Afterward, you may simply continue to observe your boss's behavior for a while or you may immediately conjure and dispatch Malgojo, so that whenever the boss speaks, he will only bury himself deeper in any of the problems caused by his vices and be unable to fend off his accusers.

Conjure any other spirits would like to help you in this situation to completely drive the boss over the edge and cause him to lose his job, however, take caution in any situation where you must be in close quarters with your enemy. You should never conjure these creatures into your home and, in many cases, your work place may be like you home away from home. So, leave the more violent spirits for situations in which you do not have much personal contact with your enemy.

The Romantic Rival

The case of the romantic rival is one in which the psychology of your enemy may figure very heavily. The more you know about him, the better you will be able to devise a successful strategy.

To illustrate, let us suppose that your romantic partner is cheating on you with a co-worker who is younger, richer and more attractive. One way to defeat such an enemy is to make him appear less attractive and sow discord between the two of them, while making yourself more attractive and desirable.

For this example, send Sangor, Turnvis, Accusael and Sheidael to your enemy.

Begin by conjuring Sangor who weakens and destroys the beauty and youth of your enemy and redirects his vital force to you for your own enhancement and increased vital energy.

Afterward, dispatch Turnvis to cause violent eruptions followed by Accusael to foster blame and distrust between your enemy and other people.

Allow these spirits do their job for a little while before delivering the final blow by sending Sheidael to cause the couple to split up.

Of course, this is just an example. If you know the personalities of the two people involved, you will be able to tailor the operation to better suit the particular circumstance.

The Business Competitor

For this example, let us suppose that you have a business selling widgets and another widget retailer has moved into your territory and is undercutting your already low prices.

In this situation, you may call upon Pernicoseuss, Gaspar and Sylex to remedy your problem.

Weaken your enemy by conjuring and dispatching Pernicoseuss to dull his senses, cause him confusion and lead him to make poor decisions.

Afterward, dispatch Gaspar to stealthily dismantle and remove your enemy's wealth a little at a time and redirect it to yourself.

Then, bring a final end to your enemy by dispatching

Sylex, a pyromaniacal demon, to finish off your competitor.

The Criminal

There is a wide variety of different types of criminals who might cause trouble for you. They should all be dealt with ruthlessly and relentlessly.

For this illustration, let us suppose you are troubled by a robber who has broken into your house, assaulted you and stolen your property. Even though you know who did it, you cannot get any help from the legal system. Moreover, because you were not only robbed but physically assaulted, you are now dealing with a lot of anxiety. Unfortunately, this is an all too common situation and one in which many people suffer in silence.

If you have any physical evidence, for example, surveillance camera footage, you may apply this using the practical method. If you got a look at your attacker, got a sense of his presence, his smell, the sound of his voice, the rhythm of his steps - whatever you have - use this memory to form an energetic pattern in your mind, which has the same energetic value as your enemy.

In such a case as this one, you might conjure and dispatch Malvader, Perilam, Rabio and finally Morbater.

For your own peace of mind and to begin your personal healing, first conjure and dispatch the rape demon, Malvader, vividly visualizing this spirit's assault on your enemy. You may send multiple instances of Malvader to your enemy to avenge you and help you regain your own strength.

Afterward, send Perilam to cause accidents and Rabio to inflict violent rage upon your enemy. Finally, send Morbater who will cooperate with Perilam and Rabio to bring your enemy to a sudden, violent end so he cannot harm other people.

Now, let us change this scenario a little bit. Suppose that your house was robbed in your absence and you did not see the thief's face nor do you have any photographic or other tangible evidence you can use. With some focus, you may use the energetic residue of this person that is lodged in your memory, which you detected when you first walked into your home and discovered it had been broken into. Mentally find resonance with this energetic imprint to locate your enemy and dispatch the little devils to him.

Disclaimer: Always perform your metaphysical work in physically safe circumstances. Do your work behind locked doors and take all precautions to secure your physical safety. Where legal matters are concerned, consult with appropriate legal experts.

THE LITTLE DEVILS

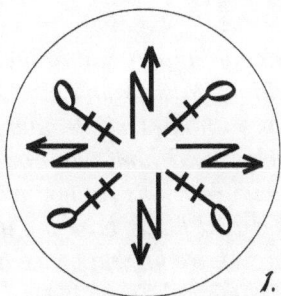

1. Desprael (Des-prah-el): A demon of suicide who appears as a black shadow self of your enemy. When this spirit possesses him, he experiences delusions and dark depression; he feels that life is so hopeless that suicide is the only way out. Desprael causes him to behave in erratic ways and commit acts, which cause him to be persecuted or rejected by those around him, including his closest friends and family members.

Incantation for Desprael: *I conjure and adjure thee, Desprael, to go to N. and by thy influence, first by whispering in his ear, then by taking control of his mind and thoughts, thou shalt bring him to his most desperate hour, so that he stands on the brink overlooking the abyss from which there is no return. Drop him into the hell of eternal torment which is his just due. I, therefore, dispatch thee, Desprael, forthwith to carry out my commands. [Insert specific command.] So be it, in the name of the Holy Tetragrammaton!*

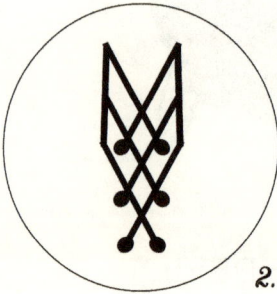

2. Fejund (Fay-yund): A vicious obsessive spirit in the form of a menacing dog that replicates itself into a pack very quickly right before the magician's eyes. Conjure Fejund to attack your enemies with vicious accusations and curse him to be mobbed and bullied by others.

Incantation for Fejund: *I conjure and adjure thee, Fejund, to go to N. and to multiply, to surround him on all sides and tear him to shreds with thy terrible, sharp teeth and claws. Let all those around him show only contempt and malice for him. Turn his allies into enemies. Lay all his weaknesses and faults bare for all to see. Allow him no pity or mercy. Give him no peace by night or day. [Insert specific command.] So be it, in the name of the Holy Tetragrammaton!*

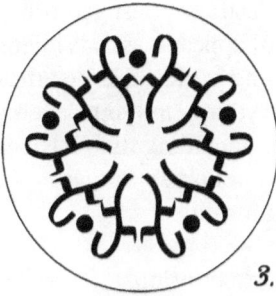

3. Gaspar (Gas-per): A demon who appears in the shape of a small, bearded man in classical Arabian raiments. Employ Gaspar to bankrupt your enemies and redirect their wealth to you.

Incantation for Gaspar: *I conjure and adjure thee, Gaspar, to go in secrecy to the dwelling of my enemy, N., and stealthily remove the wealth from him, piece by piece and bit by bit, a little at a time, and discreetly bring it here to me. [Insert specific command.] So be it, in the name of the Holy Tetragrammaton!*

4. Sylex (Sy-lex): An imp who appears engulfed in blue flames. Sylex is a fire starter, an electrical demon who burns everything in your enemy's life. Use with caution. Do not use near your own dwelling or place of business.

Incantation for Sylex: *I conjure and adjure thee, Sylex, to make haste to N. and envelop him and all he owns; destroy him and render him into a pile of char and ashes. Do thy duty and make haste! [Insert specific command.] So be it, in the name of the Holy Tetragrammaton!*

5. Streifang (Stry-fang): A destructive storm-bringer who appears as a violently reeling vortex. He decimates everything in your enemy's life, including his business, his home and his relationships.

Incantation for Streifang: *I conjure and adjure thee, Streifang, to go forthwith to N. bringing hail, lightning, high waters and powerful winds. Open up the earth beneath his feet so that he sinks into the abyss and is forever lost. [Insert specific command.] So be it, in the name of the Holy Tetragrammaton!*

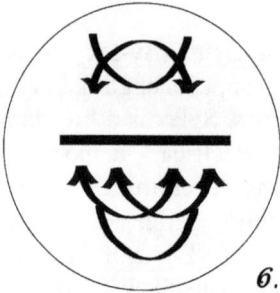

6. Malvader (Mal-vay-der): An obsessive rape demon with a curved appendage nearly as large as his torso who viciously and without cessation attacks your enemy in every orifice. Send him to punish an enemy, drive him away or torment him into compliance with your will.

Incantation for Malvader: *I conjure and adjure thee, Malvader, to go to N. and torment him day and night, torture and terrorize him and never give him any peace whether he is awake or asleep. [Insert specific command.] So be it, in the name of the Holy Tetragrammaton!*

7. Pernicoseuss (Pare-nee-co-syoos): An obsessive demon appearing in the shape of a large rodent who gnaws away at your enemy's health, gradually weakening his mind and body, thus rendering him vulnerable to *7.* other, more devastating attacks.

Incantation for Pernicoseuss: *I conjure and adjure thee, Pernicoseuss, to go to N. attach thyself to him and feed upon him, eat out his substance, lay waste to his body and debilitate his mind. Do not relent by day or night. [Insert specific command.] So be it, in the name of the Holy Tetragrammaton!*

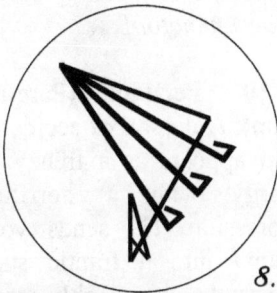

8. Malgojo (Mal-go-jo): An obsessive and possessive demon with a thick, long tongue, which he sticks down your enemy's throat, causing shortness of breath and difficulty breathing and speaking. He causes your *8.* enemy to choke on his words, lose his ability to speak with clarity and speak in opposition to his own interests.

Incantation for Malgojo: *I conjure and adjure thee, Malgojo, to go to N. and attach thyself to him, render him weak and feeble, seize his mind and body so that he speaks against his own interests whenever he opens his mouth. [Insert specific command.] So be it, in the name of the Holy Tetragrammaton!*

9. Timortus (Tim-or-tuss): An obsessive demon of worry and confusion who wears a fixed expression of horror on his face. He has four legs, six arms and a long coiling tail, with which he seizes a victim and does *9.* not let go. Send him to psychologically terrorize your enemy.

Incantation for Timortus: *I conjure and adjure thee, Timortus, to seize N. and wrap thyself around him with all the force of thy powerful limbs and tail. Whether he wakes or sleeps, by day and by night, terrorize him by thy presence, so that he is afraid of his own shadow, everyone around him and even himself. Wrack his nerves and devour his heart. [Insert specific command.] So be it, in the name of the Holy Tetragrammaton!*

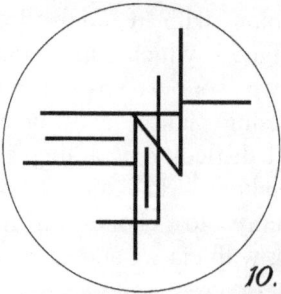

10. Perilam (Pare-ih-lahm): A demon of accidents who appears as a frenzy of energy with a horrified expression. He sends your enemy into a frantic state and renders him highly prone to accidents and other *10.* misfortunes.

Incantation for Perilam: *I conjure and adjure thee, Perilam, to go to N. and surround him with a whirl of confusion. Plague whim with misfortune and freak accidents. At every turn, place unexpected danger in his way. Give him no peace. [Insert specific command.] So be it, in the name of the Holy Tetragrammaton!*

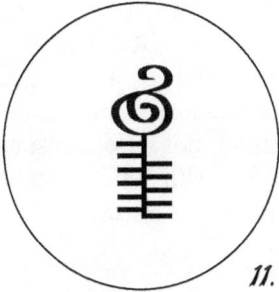

11. Malefico (Mal-ef-ee-ko): A possessive demon who appears as a shadowy creature wearing a black trench coat and a wide-brimmed black hat. He induces his host to commit all kinds of violent crimes, *11.* sets him up to get caught and encourages others to commit crimes against him.

Incantation for Malefico: *I conjure and adjure thee, Malefico, to go N. and possess him, inspire him to commit immoral acts, not in the dark of night, but in the light of day, and encourage anyone who lays eyes upon him to likewise commit crimes against him. [Insert specific command.] So be it, in the name of the Holy Tetragrammaton!*

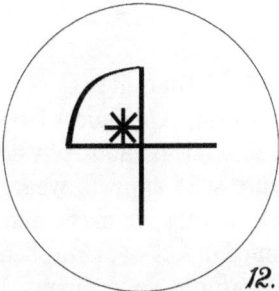

12. Morbater (Mor-bay-ter): A demon of sudden, violent death who appears in a black, hooded robe bearing a scythe in one hand and a huge hammer in the other. Send Morbater to put a quick end to an enemy.

12.

Incantation for Morbater: *I conjure and adjure thee, Morbater, to go to N. and lay a snare, let him be the victim of a tragic accident, let his worst enemies find him, let lightning strike him dead, let him be over come in an instant and cease to be on this earth. [Insert specific command.] So be it, in the name of the Holy Tetragrammaton!*

13. Rabio (Rah-bee-o): A demon of rage who appears as a shadowy three-headed, snarling dog. He consumes his host with rage and in turn inspires wrath toward him in others.

13.

Incantation for Rabio: *I conjure and adjure thee, Rabio, to go to N. obsess his body and possess his mind so that the heat of his passions overtake him and he is consumed with rage like an erupting volcano. Foster hatred, misunderstanding, envy, jealousy and frustration in him and those around him and cause them to rage against him. Cast thy dark shadow on his every undertaking, whether great or small. [Insert specific command.] So be it, in the name of the Holy Tetragrammaton!*

14. Tormuctus (Tor-muk-tuss): A demon of both psychological and physical torture who appears wearing a black robe, a mask and a pointed hood over his head. He tortures your enemy by day and night with horrors both real and imagined. Employ him to punish or dominate an enemy.

14.

Incantation for Tormuctus: *I conjure and adjure thee, Tormuctus, to go to N. and torture his mind, body and soul. Give him not peace by day or night until he complies with my will or expires. [Insert specific* *command.] So be it, in the name of the Holy Tetragrammaton!*

15. Dollus (Doll-uss): An obsessive demon of delusion and illusion who at first appears as a beautiful woman, but quickly shape-shifts into all shapes and sizes of beasts and man-beasts. He covers the eyes and ears of your enemy to prevent him from seeing the truth while injecting his own images and sounds into his host's mind. Send him to bewilder and confuse an enemy so that he always makes wrong decisions.

Incantation for Dollus: *I conjure and adjure thee, Dollus, to go to N. and dance before his eyes, seduce him with visions of grandeur, fortune, fame and whatever falsehoods suit his fancy. Deceive him, so that he deceives himself and others and so that every decision he makes is wrong, all of his endeavors are doomed to fail and all he loves crumble to dust in the wind at the touch of his hand.[Insert specific command.] So be it, in the name of the Holy Tetragrammaton!*

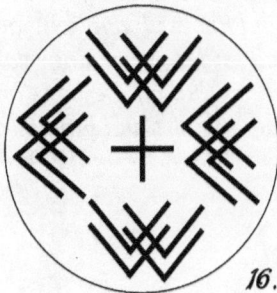

16. Pravado (Pra-va-do): A demon of unnatural desires who appears as a squat, corpulent imp wearing a lustful grin. Pravado inspires your enemy to commit lecherous acts and engage in excesses. Employ him to destroy your enemy's reputation, relationships, career and other aspects of his life.

Incantation for Pravado: I conjure and adjure thee, *Pravado, go to N. and possess his body, mind and soul and instill in him all manner of unnatural desires. If his desires are normally for women, let him desire men. Let him crave everything that is bad for him. Fill him with lust and perversity. Let him desire perverse sexual relations that lead him to his own destruction. Destroy his reputation, his health, his finances and his entire life. [Insert specific command.] So be it, in the name of the Holy Tetragrammaton!*

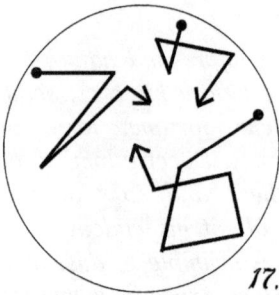

17. Difamo (Dee-fah-mo): An obsessive shape-shifting demon who first appears as a woman with talons and the tongue of a serpent. He destroys the reputation of your enemy by causing gossip, rumors and slander.

Incantation for Difamo: *I conjure and adjure thee, Difamo, to go to N. and surround him with duplicity and diabolism, besiege him on all sides, revealing dark truths and inventing deceptions, so that all the he is and all he loves is dragged down into the dirt and brought to an end. [Insert specific command.] So be it, in the name of the Holy Tetragrammaton!*

18. Malfatum (Mal-fat-um): A hideous, little imp who appears wearing ostentatious finery and brings down the powerful and mighty from high places. Employ him to bring down a powerful enemy.

18.

Incantation for Malfatum: *I conjure and adjure thee, Malfatum, to go to N., who has heretofore been fortunate in his affairs and who has friends in high places, and topple him from his high perch, ruin his reputation with both truth and slander. Reverse his good fortune, befoul his once clean mansion and send him soaring down to the lowest, filthiest place. [Insert specific command.] So be it, in the name of the Holy Tetragrammaton!*

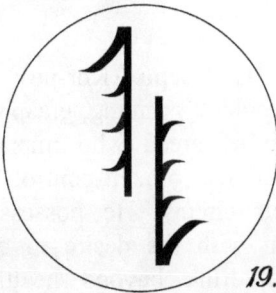

19. Sheidael (Shy-dah-el): A demon of discord who causes enmity, separation and divorce. He appears as a little imp with a long, pointed nose and an unpleasant scowl. Employ him to cause discord and strife among your enemies, thus destroying their most important and powerful alliances.

19.

Incantation for Sheidael: *I conjure and adjure thee, Sheidael, to go to N. and invade his domicile and provoke him against whoever is closest to him and them against him. Sow the seeds of enmity between them and* *divide them for ever and ever.[Insert specific command.] So be it, in the name of the Holy Tetragrammaton!*

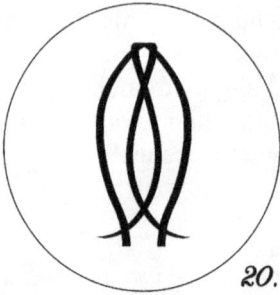

20. Gilor (Gy-lore): A demon of sexual indiscretion who appears as a drooling goblin with sharp, pointy teeth, large pointy ears and glowing black eyes. Employ him to destroy your enemy's finances, health, reputation, and relationships.

Incantation for Gilor: *I conjure and adjure thee, Gilor, to go to N. and possess him with unscrupulous and indiscriminate sexual desires and unbridled lust. Thereby, lead him surely down the path of destruction so that he suffers by disease, reputation, bad relationships, legal woes and financial difficulties. [Insert specific command.] So be it, in the name of the Holy Tetragrammaton!*

21. Corpo (Kor-po): A corpulent, grinning, grasping imp of greed who imparts wild loss of self-control to your enemy. He possesses him with the desire to eat and drink beyond healthy limitations and take things that do not belong to him.

Incantation for Corpo: *I conjure and adjure thee, Corpo, to go to N. and possess him with the desire to consume everything within his grasp, let him be insatiable so that he grows ever fatter and more greedy* *and grasping. By his greed lure him into danger and misery, let him destroy his own reputation and his own life. [Insert specific command.] So be it, in the name of the Holy Tetragrammaton!*

22. Sopvor (Sop-vor): An imp of sloth who appears clad in a black robe, yawning and stretching. He causes your enemy to lose interest in the things that once brought him pleasure, to lose his desire to be productive and eventually to lose all interest in living.

Incantation for Sopvor: *I conjure and adjure thee, Sopvor, to go to N. and render him limp and lifeless so that he is apathetic and falls into depression and poverty. Let all that he has and all that he is fall to ruin as he refuses to lift a hand or to even care. Sit on his chest and weigh him down so that he has not the strength to leave his bed. [Insert specific command.] So be it, in the name of the Holy Tetragrammaton!*

23. Stassio (Sta-see-o): A huge demon with heavy arms and legs who sits astride your enemy, immobilizing him and preventing him from taking any action against you or acting favorably on his own behalf.

Incantation for Stassio: *I conjure and adjure thee, Stassio, to go to N. and ride him, press down heavily upon him, grasp hold of his mind and fill it with paralyzing fear and worry. Give him no peace by night or day, but ride him to his death. [Insert specific command.] So be it, in the name of the Holy Tetragrammaton!*

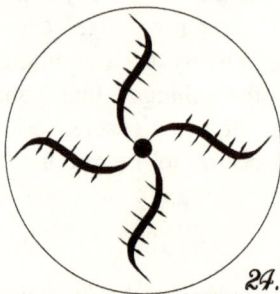

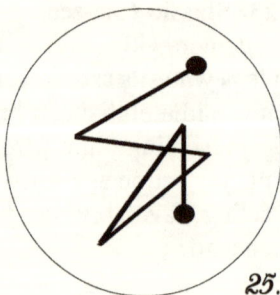

24. Mortardus (Mor-tar-duss): A large, lumbering demon who appears in the hooded, black garb of a Medieval torturer. He brings a slow, painful death to your enemy.

24.

Incantation for Mortardus: *I conjure and adjure thee, Mortardus, to go to N. and relentlessly inflict his own worst nightmares upon hm by day and night until he is overcome by the stress and strain and expires or, in desperation, dies at his own hands. [Insert specific command.] So be it, in the name of the Holy Tetragrammaton!*

25. Turnvis (Toorn-vee): A small but strong, black-bearded imp dressed in red and bearing a heavy sword who induces sudden violent rages in your enemy and those he encounters, thereby bringing about his complete destruction.

25.

Incantation for Turnvis: *I conjure and adjure thee, Turnvis, to go to N. and enrage him, cast the flames of rage upon him and stir him to a hot wrath. Let the heat of his passion spread to all those he he meets, causing them commit all manner of violence against him. Turn his own hand upon him and let him be his own undoing. [Insert specific command.] So be it, in the name of the Holy Tetragrammaton!*

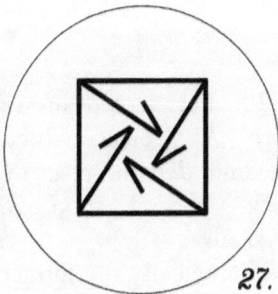

26. Sangor (San-gore): A round-headed imp with pointy ears, fangs and long arms, which he wraps around your enemy as he drains his youth and vitality and returns it to you.

Incantation for Sangor: *I conjure and adjure thee, Sangor, to go to N. and seize him, deplete every living cell of his body of its vitality and leave him an empty shell, weak, grey and waning. Cleanse his vital force and return it to me. [Insert specific command.] So be it, in the name of the Holy Tetragrammaton!*

27. Dompravus (Dom-prah-vuss): A vampirical demon who haunts a place, disturbing the inhabitants and sucking the life force out of it, leaving those who live there tired, psychologically disturbed and physically ill. Let him loose in your enemy's house or place of business to drive him out.

Incantation for Dompravus: *I conjure and adjure thee, Dompravus, to go to the home (or business) of N. and fill it with thy presence, drain all the life and happiness from this place, cause weakness, fatigue, frustration, anger, discord and despair among the inhabitants and all who go there. Sicken them and drive them out forever and ever! [Insert specific command.] So be it, in the name of the Holy Tetragrammaton!*

28. Colonius (Ko-lo-nee-us): A demon of disease, he is a tiny imp with sharp claws and horns who enters his host's body through any orifice and causes digestive problems, nausea, diarrhea, dizziness and vomiting. Your enemy who is unable to digest food or receive nourishment, eventually succumbs to a slow, miserable death.

Incantation for Colonius: *I conjure and adjure thee, Colonius, to go to N. and possess him, inflict upon him pain and humiliation, deprive his body of vital nutrients and let him slowly waste away. [Insert specific command.] So be it, in the name of the Holy Tetragrammaton!*

29. Ferracco (Fare-rok-koh): A violent, stiletto-wielding demon, clad in a black, hooded robe who physically and psychologically torments your enemy, so that he is terrorized and unable to sleep, thus progressing down a road of debilitating physical and mental illness. The first time you dispatch this spirit, do it when you believe your enemy is asleep.

Incantation for Ferracco: *I conjure and adjure thee, Ferracco, to go to N. and seize him by the throat, give him no peace, but pierce his mind and body and endlessly torment him. When he desires sleep do not permit it, but visit nightmares upon him and violently stir him awake. When he wishes to stay awake, force his eyes closed. Whisper with strange voices in his ears and play illusions before his eyes by day and night until he goes mad. [Insert specific command.] So be it, in the name of the Holy Tetragrammaton!*

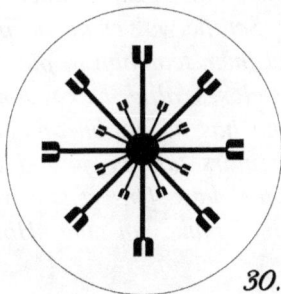

30.

30. Muticus (Mew-tee-cuss): An imp of silence, powerfully built with large, strong hands, who seizes the tongue of your enemy and renders him unable to communicate effectively. Employ him to silence a gossip or anyone speaking against you. In legal proceedings, he may be employed against an opposing lawyer or witness.

Incantation for Muticus: *I conjure and adjure thee, Muticus, to go to N. and seize his tongue, render him speechless, restrain him, stiffen his muscles of speech, render them useless and silence him forever. [Insert specific command.] So be it, in the name of the Holy Tetragrammaton!*

31. Accusael (Ach-koo-zah-el): An imp who appears in the classic form of the devil, like a wicked judge in a black robe and barrister's wig. He inspires brutality and corruption in government officials and *31.* causes your enemy to be plagued by legal problems and to be persecuted by members of law enforcement agencies.

Incantation for Accusael: *I conjure and adjure thee, Accusael, to go to N. and accuse him of all manner of evil whether it be true or false. Set the wolves in sheep's clothing upon his heels and let them tear him to pieces in their thirst for blood. Let his closest allies betray him. Let him be a marked man who has no nation and no home. Let him flee his persecutors and be forced to wander alone for the rest of his days. [Insert specific command.] So be it, in the name of the Holy Tetragrammaton!*

32. Kreager (Kree-ger): A warrior demon who lays siege to your enemy on all fronts. He appears as a short, squat, horned creature wearing a helmet and bearing a rucksack over his shoulder. He sacks your *32.* enemy's possessions and siphons his wealth to you.

Incantation for Kreager: *I conjure and adjure thee, Kreager, to go to N., cause him trouble and strife and deprive him of all his worldly goods. Replace his wealth with poverty and bring his fortune to me. [Insert specific command.] So be it, in the name of the Holy Tetragrammaton!*

33. Strangulo (Strang-gew-lo): A dark imp with long fingers who wears a devious grin. He chokes your enemy while he is sleeping, speaking or eating, eventually resulting in his demise.

33.

Incantation for Strangulo: *I conjure and adjure thee, Strangulo, to go to N. and wrap thy sinewy fingers tightly around his throat. Strangle him in his bed, so that whenever he drifts off to sleep he quickly wakes, choking and unable to breathe. When he speaks, tighten thy grasp so that he chokes on his own words. Let him choke on even the tiniest morsel. Leave him no peace by night or day. [Insert specific command.] So be it, in the name of the Holy Tetragrammaton!*

THE GUARDIANS

The guardians are spirits of the same class of being as the first 33 who serve and protect you from the machinations of your enemies and from any of the little devils you have dispatched who might go rogue or try to return to you. Essentially, they are familiar spirits whom you must feed once per week to maintain their service.

How To Summon and Maintain the Guardians

Place a piece of red cotton or wool cloth in the bottom a small box with a lid. Using a pen with black ink, trace each of the three sigils of the guardians onto small pieces of clean parchment or white paper. Then, place the papers into the box.

Prepare a solution of a small amount of whiskey (approximately 2 ounces or 60 milliliters) mixed with a few drops of your own blood to feed your guardians and link them to you. Place this formula in a small bottle with a lid and label it accordingly.

Go into a meditative state. Then, summon and feed each guardian in succession, by reciting his incantation and sprinkling a few drops of the solution onto the cloth.

As you recite each incantation, visualize the being according to its description, coming to you, feeding from the blood and whiskey, receiving any command you give him and then departing to perform his duty.

To maintain their service, repeat the procedure of summoning and feeding each of them once per week. Just as with the first 33 spirits, you may include special commands for each of them, if you have any.

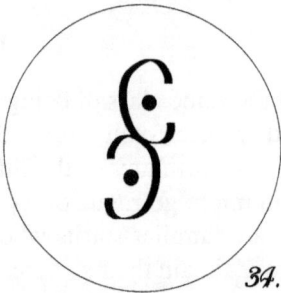

34. Nocculos (Nok-u-loss) An owlish-looking imp with round, unblinking, yellow eyes who acts as a lookout and a reporter. He brings you information about your operations. He, also, shrouds you and your interests in darkness, obscuring your private activities. By calling upon Nocculos, you may receive a report about your enemies and the progress of your operations by commanding him to give you this information.

Incantation for Nocculos: *I conjure and adjure thee, Nocculos, that thou wilt serve me and come forthwith when I call and present thyself with all obedience and humility. I charge thee to be my eyes in the night and to report to me all activity relevant to me and my endeavors. [Insert specific command.] So be it, in the name of the Holy Tetragrammaton!*

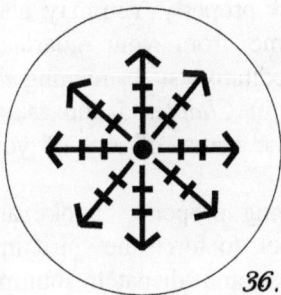

35. Sicrael (Sik-ra-el) The demon-slayer who appears as a sword-bearing man with the face of a dog. He goes out to survey the spirits and destroys entities who go rogue or try to return to you to.

Incantation for Sicrael: *I conjure and adjure thee, Sicrael, that thou wilt serve me and come forthwith when I call and present thyself with all obedience and humility. I charge thee to destroy any entity who should defy my orders. [Insert specific command.] So be it, in the name of the Holy Tetragrammaton!*

36. Pratael (Pray-tah-el) The personal defender who appears in the form of a snarling, horned, black panther. He stays close to you and your home to fend off any attacks on you, your dwelling or your interests.

Incantation for Pratael: *I conjure and adjure thee, Pratael, that thou wilt serve me and come forthwith when I call and present thyself with all obedience and humility. I charge thee to defend me, my property and all my interests from all intruders. [Insert specific command.] So be it, in the name of the Holy Tetragrammaton!*

Managing a Psychic Attack

In a small journal, keep a record of the spirits you dispatch, when and where. Each incantation allows you to optionally insert specific commands for the spirit; any such commands should be written down and kept as part of your records. Keep your journal away from prying eyes.

Secrecy is very important for the success of this kind of work, which is designed to cause misery and possibly even death to an enemy. Your efforts could be thwarted and you could be subject to retaliation, if your enemy discovers that he is under attack. At the very least, he might take steps to remove the spirits, thus derailing the operation.

To ensure that the spirit is doing his job, go into a meditative state, mentally locate your enemy and observe if he is doing his work properly. You may, also, request a report at any time from your guardian, Nocculos, by going into a meditative state, reciting the incantation for him provided in *Chapter 5* and asking him for information about the status of any of your operations.

If an entity is not behaving properly, invoke and dispatch your guardian, Sicrael, to force the spirit into compliance. You may invoke and dispatch multiple instances of a particular entity or employ any combination of spirits against your enemy at any time during the course of an operation.

How to Stop an Operation

Never dispatch these entities on a mere whim. An operation can be aborted, but it is not ideal to do so.

To stop an operation, dispatch the destroyer, Sicrael, with instructions to terminate each entity you have previously dispatched by name, in reverse order. Consult your journal to determine the names of the entities and the order in which they were dispatched.

Incantation to terminate an operation: *I conjure and adjure thee, Sicrael, that thou shalt find and destroy N. [Insert specific command.] So be it, in the name of the Holy Tetragrammaton.*

If you have bound the demons sigil with the personal effect of the enemy, then these things should be unbound, held under running water and then buried at the base of a tree off your property.

Be advised that simply stopping an operation will not reverse any harm the little devils have already caused.

OTHER WINTER TEMPEST BOOKS

If you enjoyed this book, you might enjoy other Winter Tempest Books:

All Natural Dental Remedies: Herbs and Home Remedies to Heal Your Teeth & Naturally Restore Tooth Enamel by Angela Kaelin

Black Magic for Dark Times: Spells of Revenge and Protection by Angela Kaelin (Fiction)

Blood and Black Roses: A Dark Bouquet of Vampires, Romance and Horror by Sophia diGregorio (Fiction)

The Forgotten: The Vampire Prince by Sophia diGregorio (Fiction)

Grimoire of Santa Muerte: Spells and Rituals of Most Holy Death, the Unofficial Saint of Mexico by Sophia diGregorio

How to Communicate with Spirits: Séances, Ouija Boards and Summoning by Angela Kaelin

How to Develop Advanced Psychic Abilities: Obtain Information about the Past, Present and Future Through Clairvoyance by Sophia diGregorio

How to Read the Tarot for Fun, Profit and Psychic Development by Angela Kaelin

How to Write Your Own Spells for Any Purpose and Make Them Work by Sophia diGregorio

Magical Healing:How to Use Your Mind to Heal Yourself and Others by Angela Kaelin

Natural Remedies for Reversing Gray Hair: Nutrition and Herbs for Anti-aging and Optimum Health by Thomas W. Xander

Practical Black Magic: How to Hex and Curse Your Enemies by Sophia diGregorio

Spells for Money and Wealth by Angela Kaelin

To Conjure the Perfect Man by Sophia diGregorio (Fiction)

The Traditional Witches' Book of Love Spells by Angela Kaelin

Traditional Witches' Formulary and Potion-making Guide: Recipes for Magical Oils, Powders and Other Potions by Sophia diGregorio

ABOUT THE AUTHOR

Angela Kaelin is the author of metaphysical books, such as, *How to Communicate with Spirits: Séances, Ouija Boards and Summoning, The Traditional Witches' Book of Love Spells, Spells for Money and Wealth,* and *Magical Healing: How to Use Your Mind to Heal Yourself and Others.* She is, also, an alternative health writer and the author of *All Natural Dental Remedies: Herbs and Home Remedies to Heal Your Teeth & Naturally Restore Tooth Enamel.*

Disclaimer: The author and publisher of this guide has used her best efforts in preparing this document. The author makes no representation or warranties with respect to the accuracy, applicability, fitness or completeness of the contents of this document. The author disclaims any warranties expressed or implied. The author of this book is not a medical or legal professional and is not qualified to give medical or legal advice. Nothing in this document should be construed as medical or legal advice. The material in this book is presented for informational purposes only. The procedures described in this book should not be used a substitute for treatment from state approved, licensed medical authorities.

Nothing in this book should be construed as incitement to dangerous or illegal acts and the reader is advised to be aware of and heed all pertinent laws in his or her city, state, country or other jurisdiction. Any medical or legal questions should be addressed to the proper medical or legal authorities. The author shall in no event be held liable for any losses or damages, including but not limited to special, incidental, consequential or other damages incurred by the use of this information. Always take proper precautions with candles, sharp objects, essential oils, herbs and use only as directed.

The statements in this book have not been evaluated by any other government entity. The statements contained herein represent the legally protected opinions of the author and are presented for informational purposes only. Anyone who uses any of the information in the book does so at their own risk with the understanding that the author cannot be held responsible for the consequences.

FTC Disclaimer: The author has no connection to nor was paid by any brand or product described in this document with the exception of any other books mentioned which were written by the author or published by Winter Tempest Books.

Copyright: This document contains material protected under copyright laws. Any unauthorized reprint, transmission or resale of this material without the express permission of the author is strictly prohibited.